Chet Baker

Play-Along

10 compositions by Wolfgang Lackerschmid
10 transcriptions of the original Chet Baker solos in C and B♭

The original compositions were released on

Chet Baker/Wolfgang Lackerschmid

BALLADS FOR TWO
(CD inak 856 CD)

Chet Baker/Wolfgang Lackerschmid

ORIGINALS
(CD asj 001)

Chet Baker/Wolfgang Lackerschmid

WELCOME BACK
(CD West Wind 2083)

Chet Baker/Wolfgang Lackerschmid

feat. Larry Coryell/Buster Williams/Tony Williams
(CD inak 857 CD)

Solo transcriptions by Wolfgang Lackerschmid, except "Welcome Back" by Barbara Gilglberger
Enharmonic correction by Reinhold Bauer

TABLE OF CONTENTS

chet baker *play along*

© 1996 by ADVANCE Music

All Rights Reserved

Music typesetting & layout: Hans-Jörg Rüdiger

Cover design: 10eg

Printed by Wega-Verlag, Mainz

Production: Hans Gruber

Order # 01107

Waltz For Berlin

Wolfgang Lackerschmid

C

Chet Baker's solo on the chord changes to

Waltz For Berlin

Gloria's Answer

Wolfgang Lackerschmid

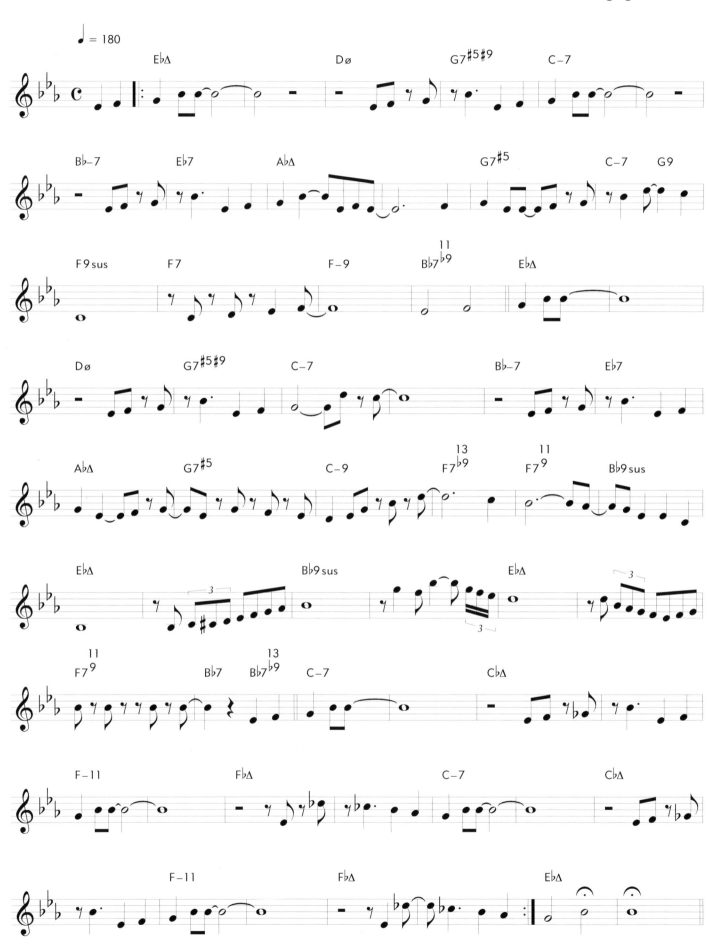

Chet Baker's solo on the chord changes to

Gloria's Answer

Gloria's Answer

C

Try It Dry

Wolfgang Lackerschmid

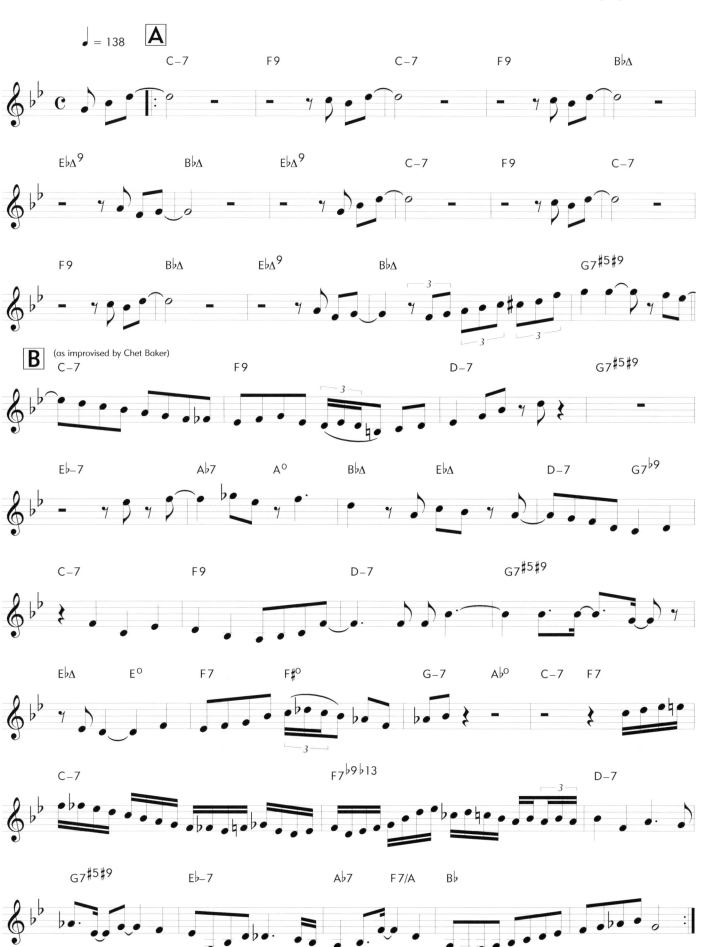

Volta Trais
(Waiting For A Change)

Wolfgang Lackerschmid

1) I've been wai - ting for a change in the air, for a
2) I'm look - ing for a change in the sky, for a

sign from a far off spring.
moon that is meant for me.

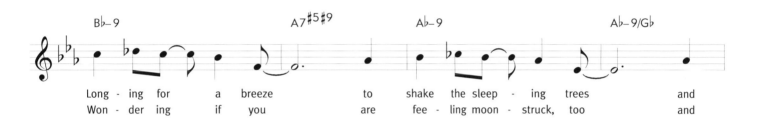

Long - ing for a breeze to shake the sleep - ing trees and
Won - der ing if you are fee - ling moon - struck, too and

hop - ing love is what the breeze will bring
hop - ing that you un - der - stand that (I've been waiting for a change)

Chet Baker's solo on the chord changes to
Volta Trais

Balzwaltz

Wolfgang Lackerschmid

C

Chet Baker's solo as sung on the chord changes to

Balzwaltz

Pitztal Daybreak

Wolfgang Lackerschmid

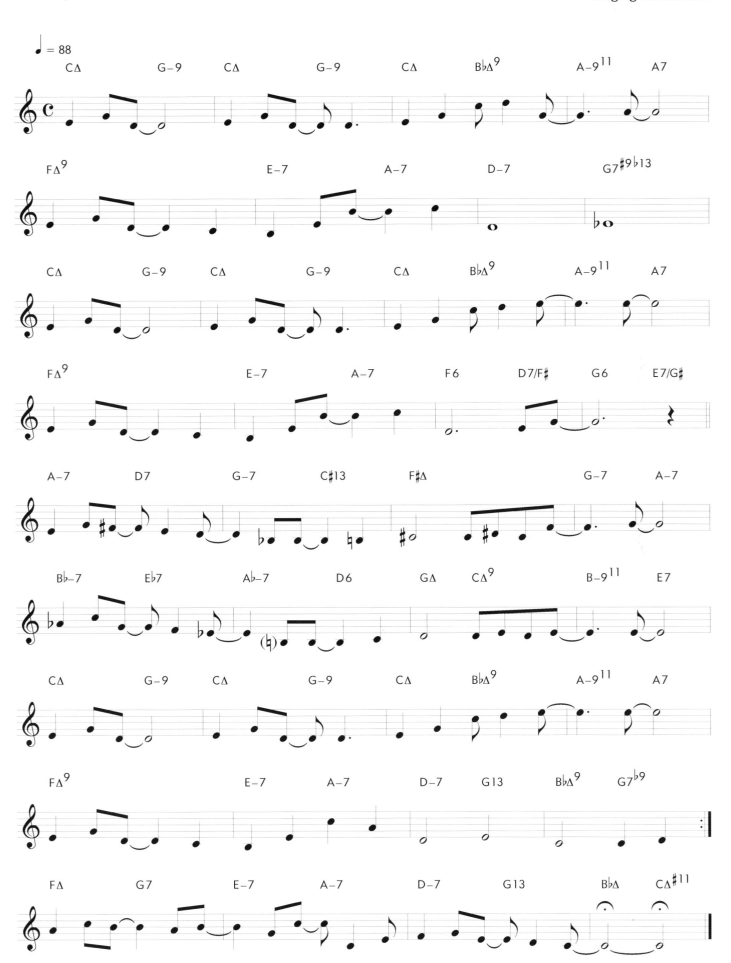

Chet Baker's solo on the chord changes to

Pitztal Daybreak

Waltz For Susan

Wolfgang Lackerschmid

C

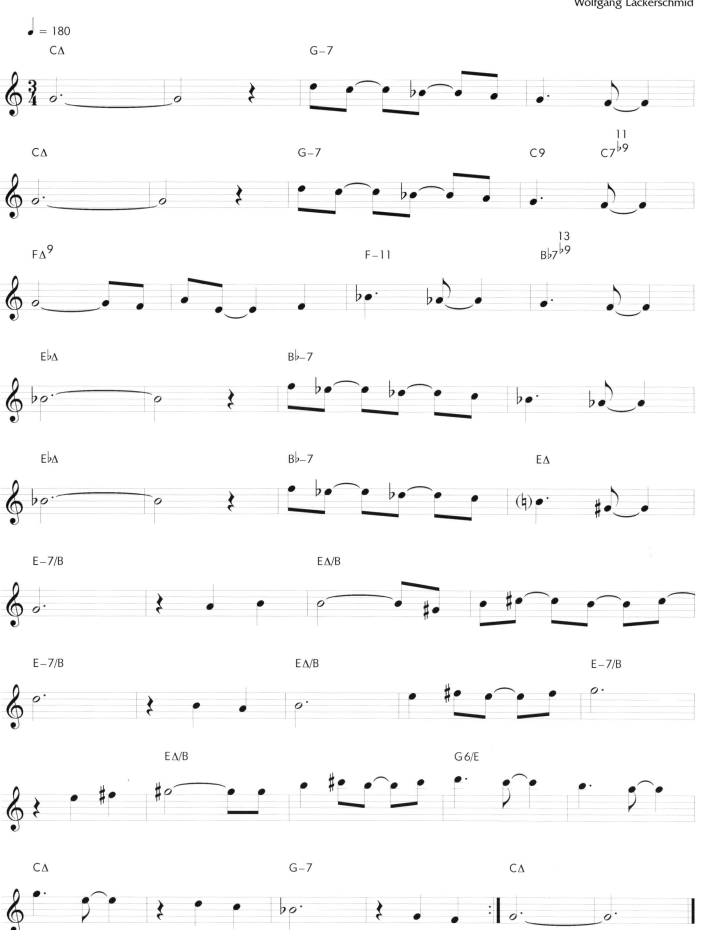

Chet Baker's solo on the chord changes to
Waltz For Susan

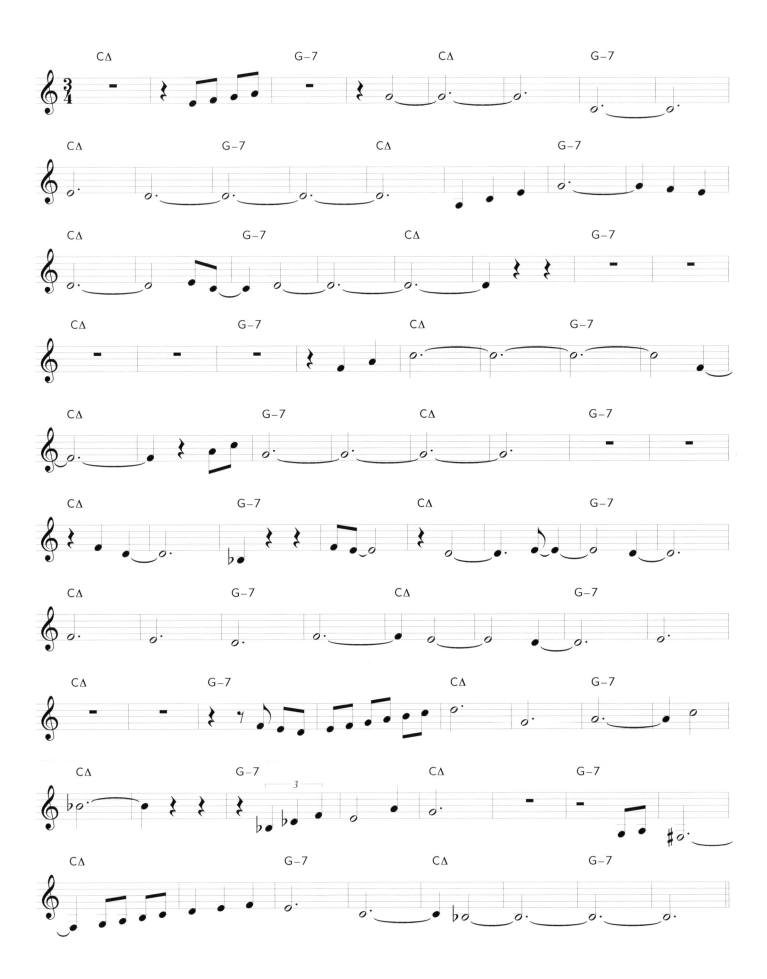

Christmas Waltz

Wolfgang Lackerschmid

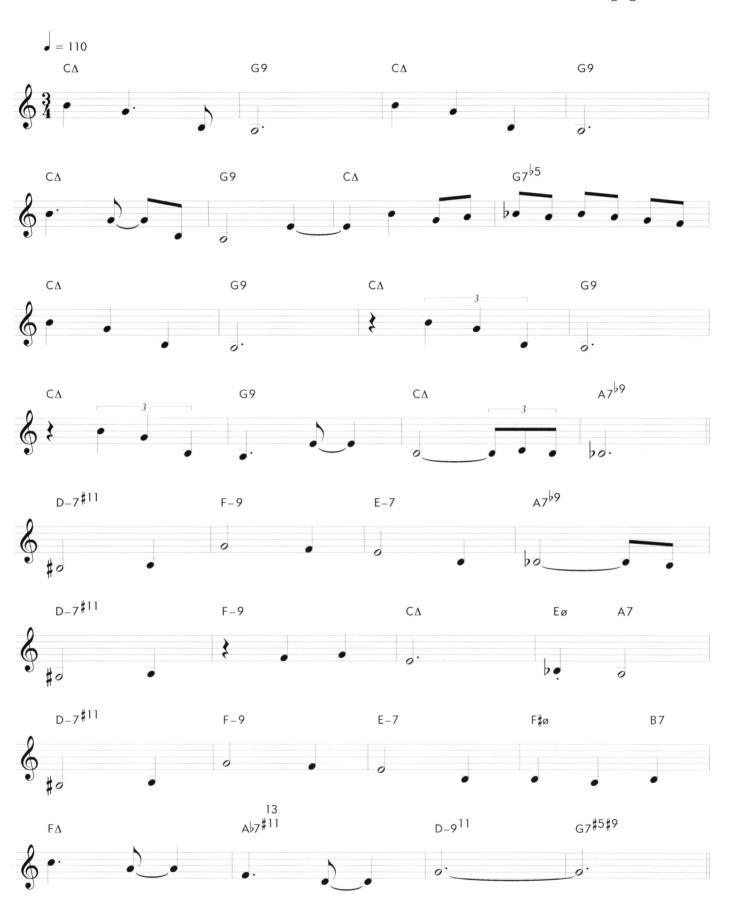

Chet Baker's solo on the chord changes to

Christmas Waltz

Welcome Back
Lyrics by Tricia Tunstall

Wolfgang Lackerschmid

1) Wel- come back from   far   a - way!   Knew that you were gon - na be   back some - day.
2) Wel- come back from   a - ny- where!   Were you e - ver dream - in of   me   out there?

You've been trav' - lin'   fast and free,   now   at last you're tra - ve - lin'   back   to me.
While   you sailed the   o - pen sea,   did   you think of   tra - ve - lin'   back   to me?

Ba - by, I don't need to know who was sad when you said you had to go.
Ba - by, I can wan - der too, but you know I'll be wand'r - in' back to you.

I'm   just glad I'm   here   to   wel - come you home.
Hop - in' you'll be   there   to   wel - come me home.

(And may - be there will come a   day we'll both be com - in' back to   stay.)   Wel- come!

Chet Baker's solo on the chord changes to

Welcome Back

Why Shouldn't You Cry

Lyrics by Tricia Tunstall (dedicated to Chet, 1993)

Wolfgang Lackerschmid

Chet Baker's solo on the chord changes to

Why Shouldn't You Cry

C

Chet Baker & Wolfgang Lackerschmid

Photos: Hans Kumpf

Waltz For Berlin

Wolfgang Lackerschmid

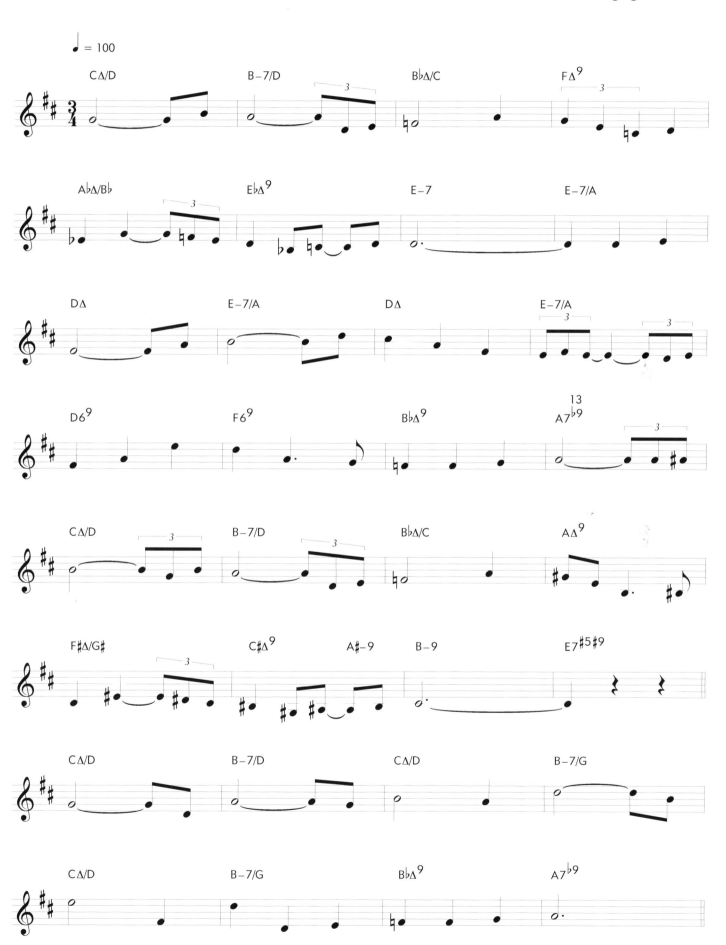

Chet Baker's solo on the chord changes to

Waltz For Berlin

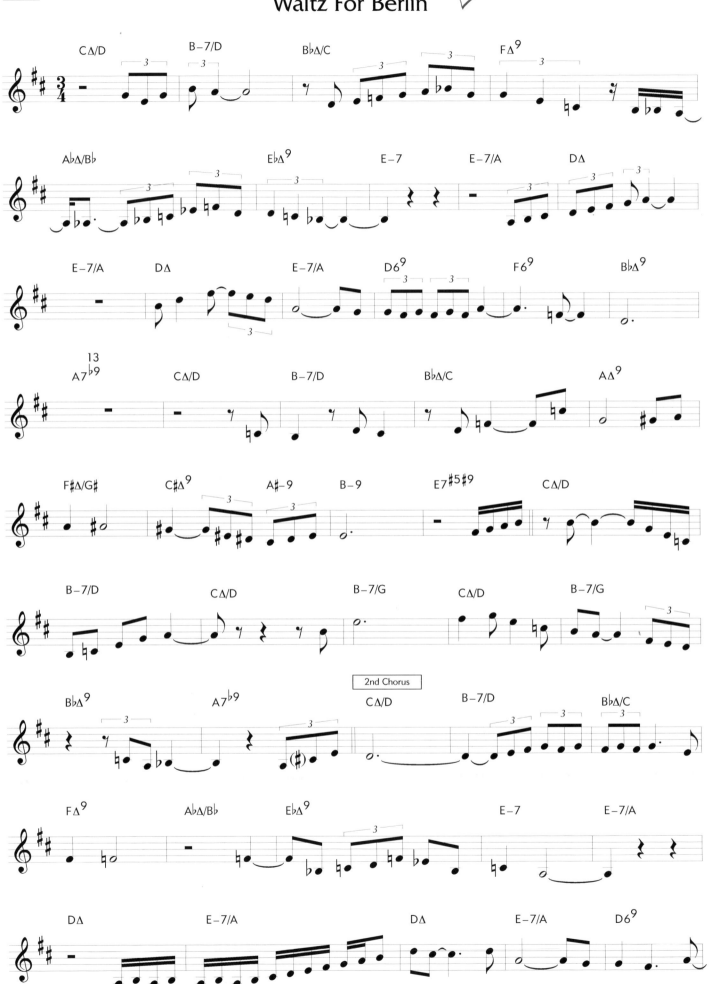

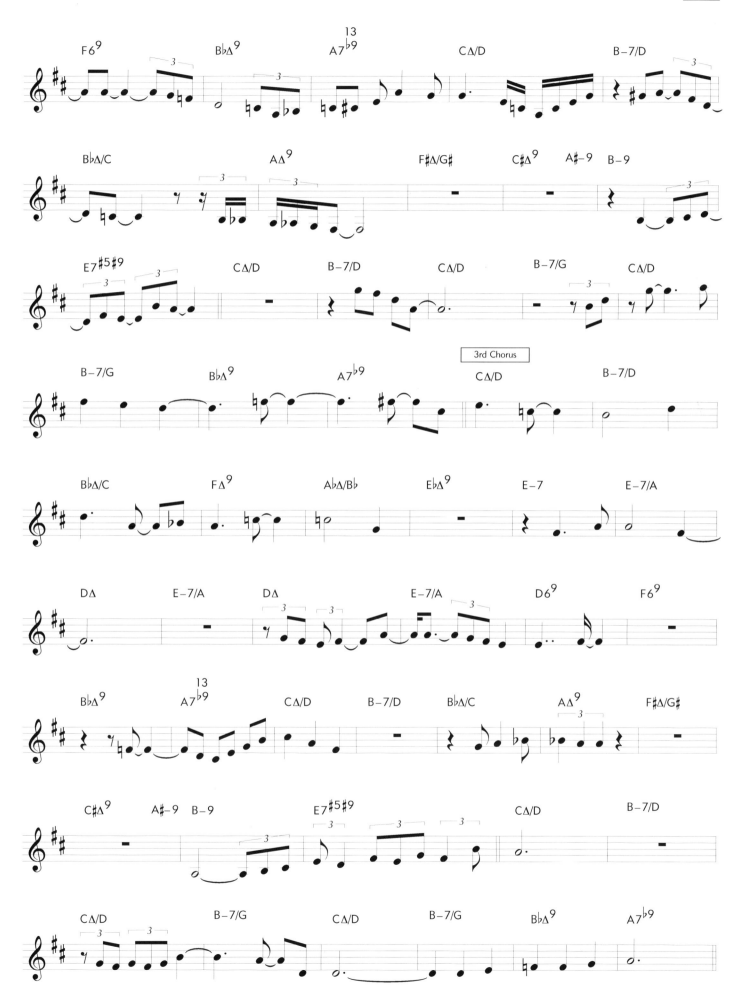

Gloria's Answer

Wolfgang Lackerschmid

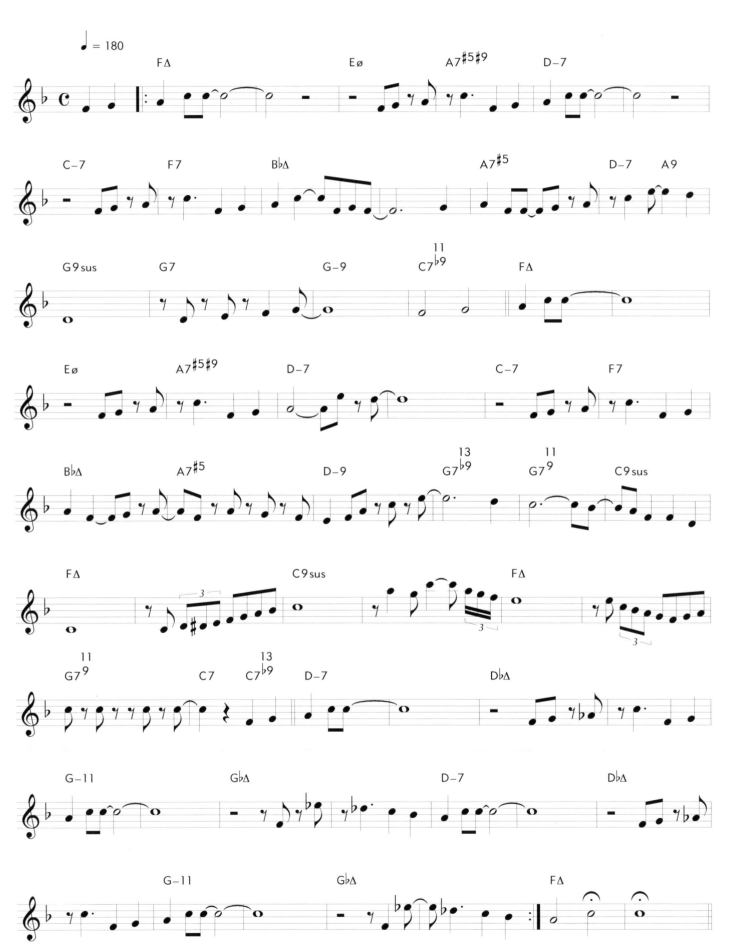

Chet Baker's solo on the chord changes to

Gloria's Answer

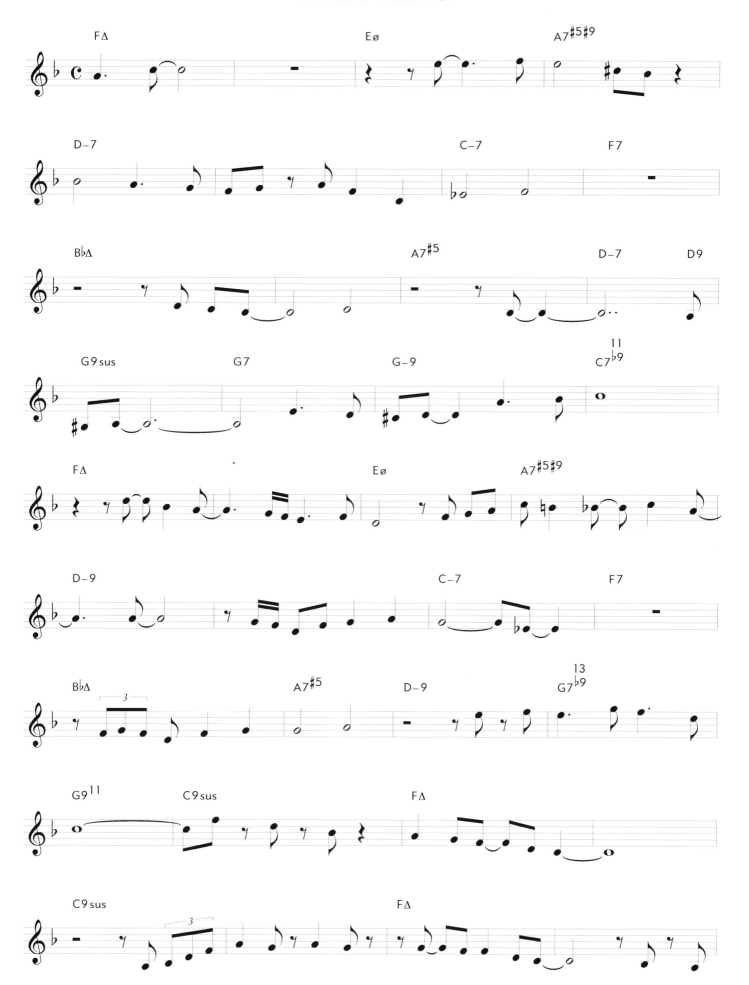

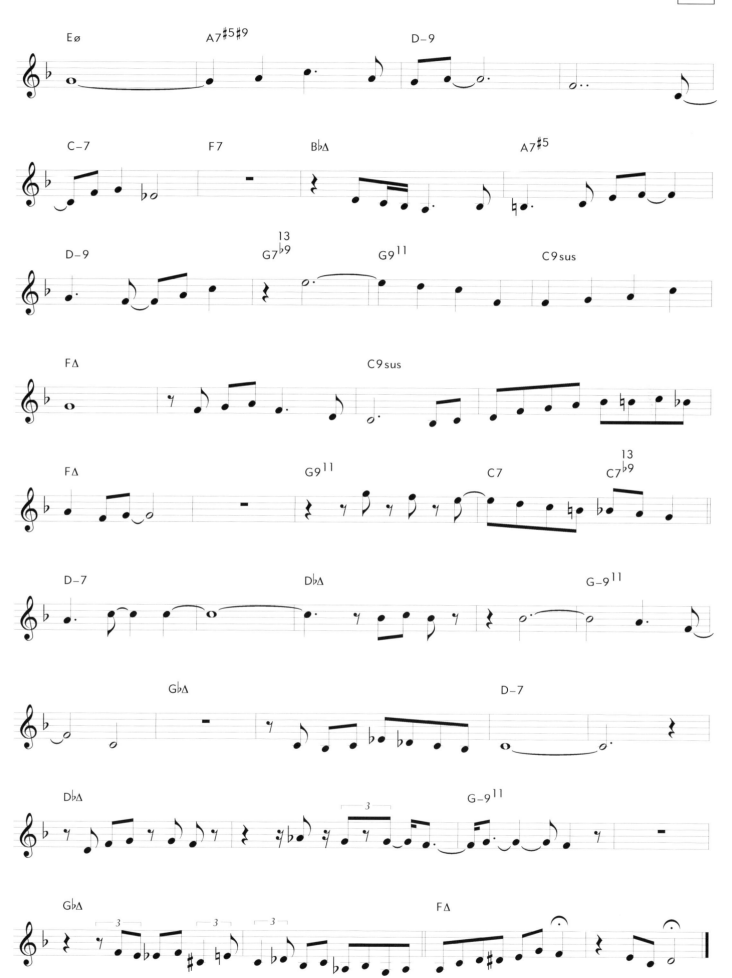

Try It Dry

Wolfgang Lackerschmid

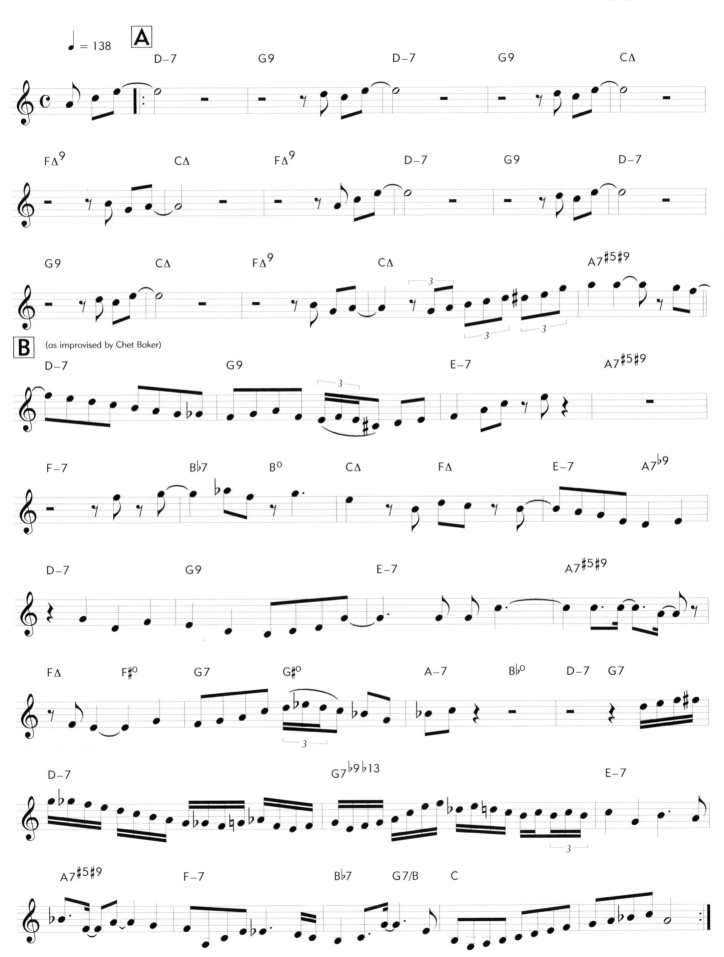

Volta Trais
(Waiting For A Change)

Wolfgang Lackerschmid

(see the "C concert" section for lyrics)

Chet Baker's solo on the chord changes to

Volta Trais

Balzwaltz

Wolfgang Lackerschmid

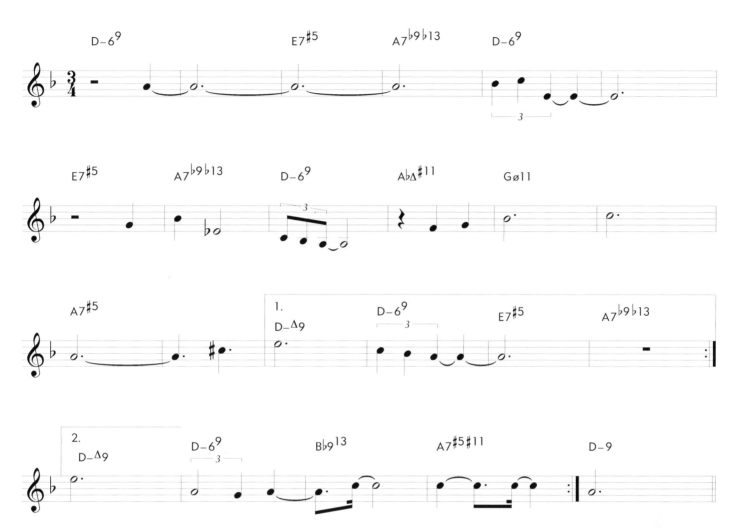

© 1993 SILVANUS Musikverlag

Balzwaltz

Pitztal Daybreak

Wolfgang Lackerschmid

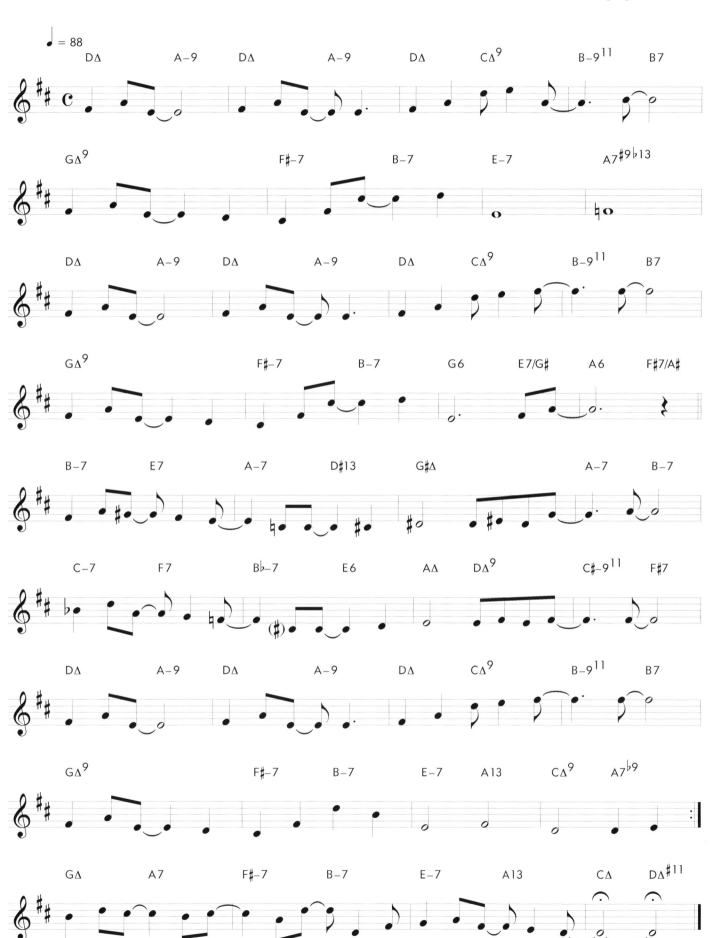

Pitztal Daybreak

Waltz For Susan

Bb

Wolfgang Lackerschmid

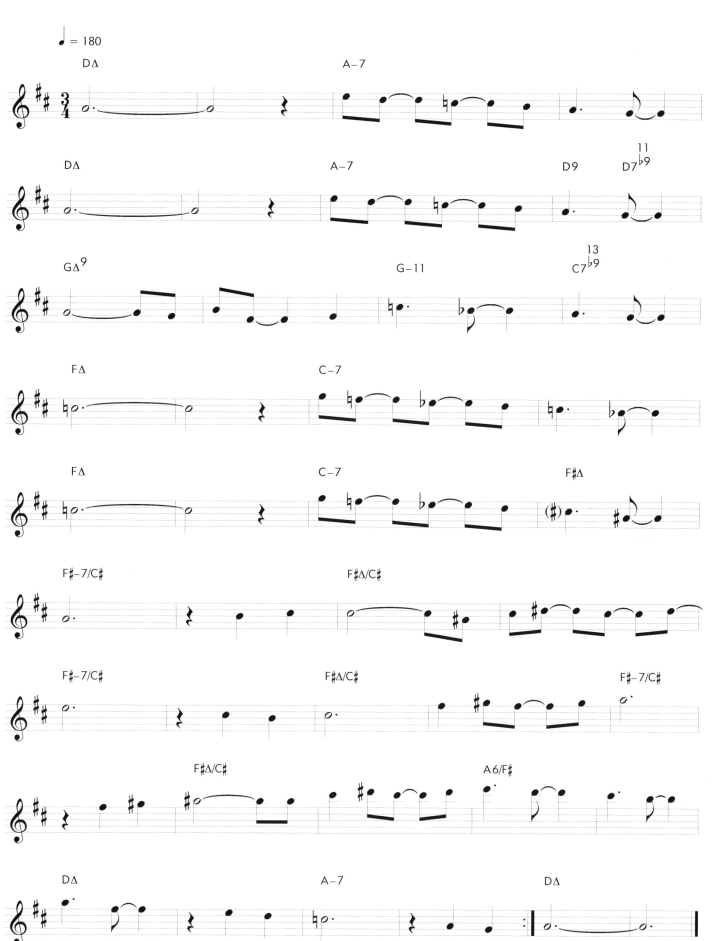

Waltz For Susan

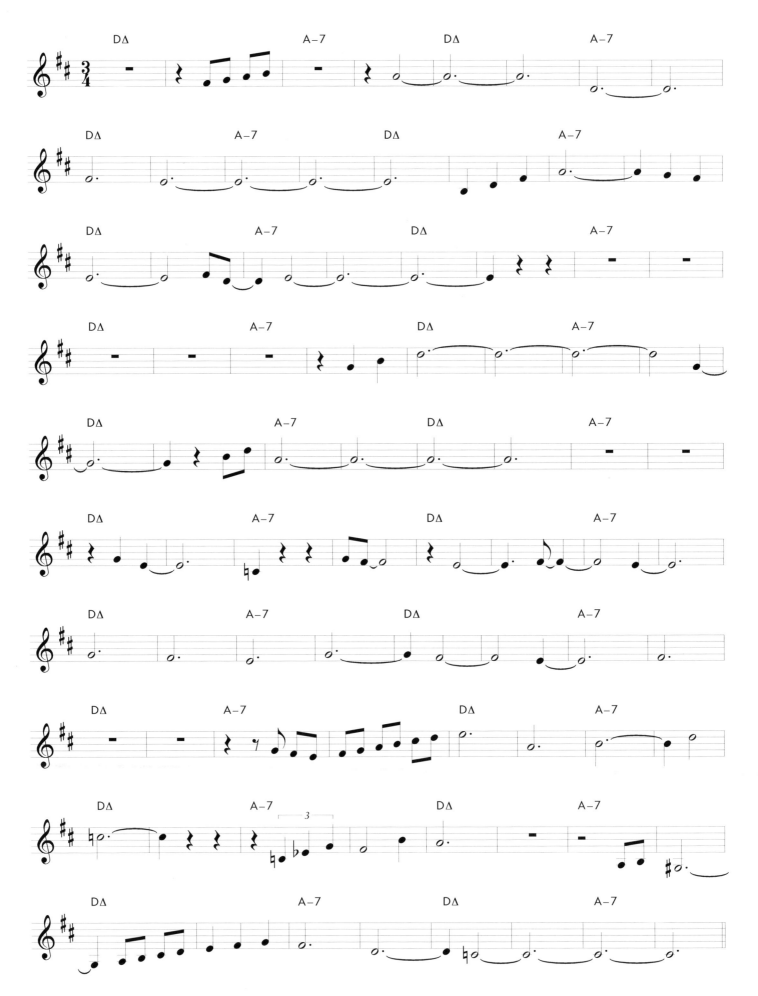

Christmas Waltz

Wolfgang Lackerschmid

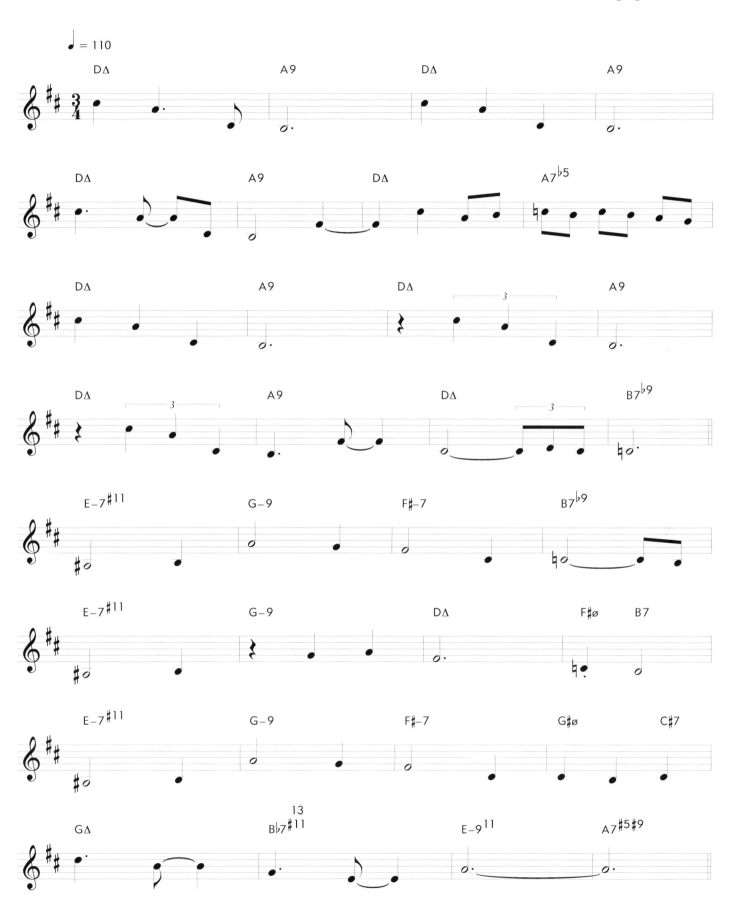

B♭

Chet Baker's solo on the chord changes to
Christmas Waltz

Welcome Back

Wolfgang Lackerschmid

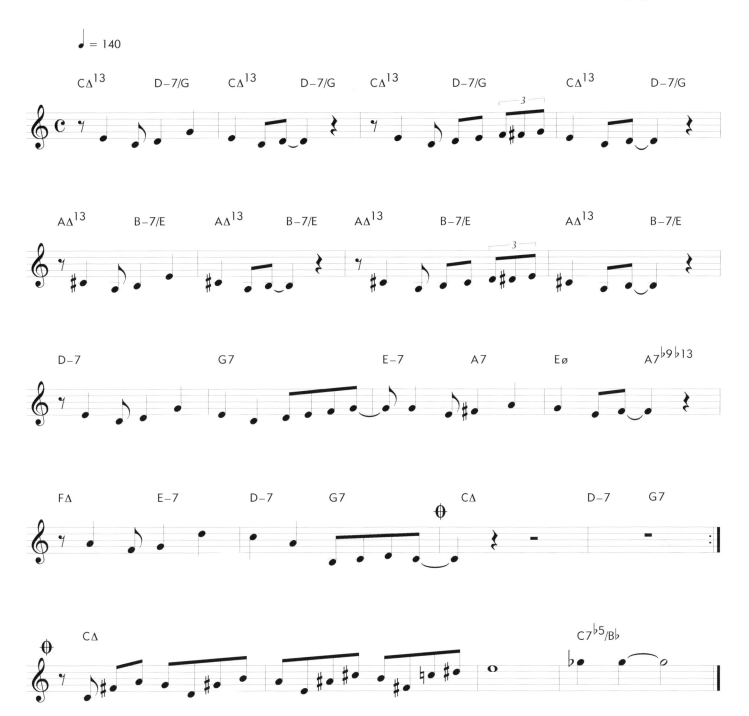

(see the "C concert" section for lyrics)

Chet Baker's solo on the chord changes to

Welcome Back

Why Shouldn't You Cry

Wolfgang Lackerschmid

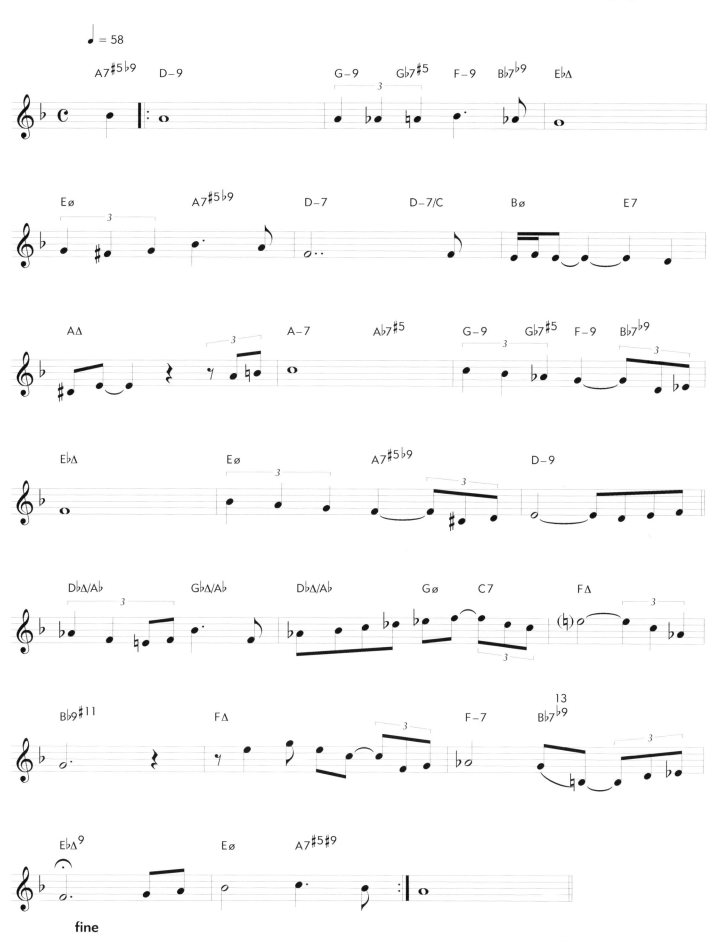

fine

(see the "C concert" section for lyrics)

Why Shouldn't You Cry

B♭